Shadows on Hadrian's Wall

A Poetic Journey along the Wall

John S. Langley

Copyright © 2022 J. S.langley

The right of J. S. Langley to be identified as the Author of the Work has been asserted by them in accordance Copyrights, Designs and Patents Act 1988.
The Copyright for each poem resides with the author. All images are the property of the author or or freely available in the public domain.

First Published in 2022 by LV Publishing 2022

Apart from any use permitted under UK copyright law, this publication may only be reproduced, stored in a retrieval system, or transmitted, in any form, or by any means, with prior permission in writing of the publisher or, in the case of reprographic production, in accordance with the terms of licenses issued by the Copyright Licensing Agency.

All characters and events in this publication, other than those clearly in the public domain, are fictitious and any resemblance to real persons, living or dead, is purely coincidental.

Print ISBN: 978-1-7391381-1-0

To Those who mean a lot to me

Thanks

And to all the people whose names are not recorded but were there - the now silent majority.

John S. Langley

CONTENTS

I. Ravenglass (Glannoventa)   Page
   1. Red Dawn   3
   2. Safe Harbour   4
   3. When   5

II. Moresby (Gabosentum)
   4. Moon and Clouds   8
   5. Feelings on Arrival   9

III. Burrow Walls (Magis)
   6. Strangers   12
   7. Letter Home   13
   8. gods   15

IV. Maryport (Alavna Carvetiorvm)
   9. Snowdrops   18
   10. Power   19

V. Beckfoot (Bibra)
   11. Mistletoe   22
   12. Mizpah   23

VI. Bowness-on-Solway (Maia)
   13. Me, The Wall   26
   14. Pax Romana?   29
   15. Solway   30
   16. First to last   31

VII. Drumburgh (Coggabata)

    17. Curlew   34
    18. Eagles   35
    19. Birrus Britannicus   36
    20. Your Wall Needs You!   37

VIII. Burgh by Sands (Aballava)

    21. Vallum   40
    22. Real Life I   41
    23. A Turn of Events   43
    24. Haaf Fishing   44

IX. Stanwix/Carlisle(Uxelodunum/Luguvalium)

    25. Samhain   48
    26. Tideline   50
    27. Fire   52
    28. Seasonal Blood-Letting   53
    29. Mary Queen of Scots   54

X. Castlesteads (Camboglanna)

    30. Lanercost   58
    31. Woods   59
    32. Honey Bees   60
    33. Reivers   61

XI. Banks Turret

    34. Turret Truth   64

XII. Birdoswald (Banna)

35. Dinner Party	68
36. Winter's Heroes	69
37. Stones I	74
38. Brown Trout	75

XIII. Bewcastle (Fanum Cocidi)

39. Bewcastle Cross	78
40. Jeopardy	79

XIV. Carvoran (Magna)

41. Scars on the Land	82
42. Settling	83
43. Recycling	84
44. Regrets	85

XV. Great Chesters (Aesica)

45. Water	88
46. Windhover	89
47. Hard Frost	90
48. Night Watch	91
49. Under Attack	92

XVI. Chesterholm (Vindolanda)

50. Wolves	96
51. Beer	98
52. Messaging	99
53. Husband's Offering	100
54. Real Life II	101
55. The Dig	102

XVII. Milecastle 37

    56. On Duty   106

XVIII. Housesteads (Vercovicium)

    57. Whin Sill   110
    58. Cold on the Wall   111
    59. Collecting Debts   112
    60. Outside the Gates   113
    61. Skin Deep   114
    62. A Night at Twice Brewed   115

XIX. Carrawburgh (Brocolitia)

    63. Stones II   120
    64. Military Zone   121
    65. Altar   122
    66. Different Outcomes   123
    67. Coventina's Well   125

XX. (Walwick) Chesters (Cilurnum)

    68. Foundations   130
    69. Strongroom   131
    70. Central Heating   132
    71. Human vs Machine   133
    72. Heavenfield   134
    73. Let slip the Dogs   135

XXI. High Rochester (Bremenium)

    74. Loads of Loaves   138
    75. Picts   139
    76. Crows   140

XXII. Corbridge (Coria)

    77. Wanderer   144
    78. Blacksmith   145
    79. Entertainment I   146
    80. Snipping   147
    81. Ketchup   148
    82. Market Day   149
    83. The Veteran   150
    84. Entertainment II   152

XXIII. Haltonchesters (Onnum)

    85. Bordering   156
    86. Northern Lights   158
    87. The Source   159
    88. Cramp   160
    89. Manoeuvres   162
    90. Meeting with Ghosts   163

XXIV. Rudchester (Vindobala)

    91. The Good Times   166
    92. Used Coins   168
    93. Woad   169
    94. Snow   171
    95. Storm   172
    96. Merlin   174

XXV. Benwell (Hill) (Condercum)

    97. A Request   178
    98. The Farmer   179
    99. The Auxiliary   180
    100. Witching Hours   181

XXVI. Newcastle upon Tyne (Pons Aelius)

101.	Population Explosion	184
102.	Bureaucrat	186
103.	A Mother's Prayer	188
104.	The Wind	189
105.	The interview	190
106.	Pilgrimages	191
107.	On Their Shoulders	192

XXVII. Wallsend (Segedunum)

108.	Father to Son	196
109.	Alienation	197
110.	Wall's End	198
111.	What's in a Name	199
112.	21st Century Travel	201
113.	Will?	202

XXVIII. Jarrow (Roman Name Unknown)

114.	Language	206
115.	Formulae	207
116.	Omens	208
117.	Marsh Dwellers	209

XXIX. South Shields (Arbeia)

118.	Granary at Night	216
119.	Luck and Fate	217
120.	Picking over the Ruins	218
121.	North Sea Coast	219
122.	Red Sky	220

Note:

I have included some notes along the way but I must say right from the outset that I am no expert and this collection is in no way meant to be an authoritative guide.

The notes are meant to lightly trace the steps we take along the way and give a flavour of people, place and time; to suggest sights, and sounds and smells.

Any errors (however accidental) are all my own.

John S. Langley

Shadows on the Wall

Speak Wall
Speak stones
Tell of the years
The people you've known

Stand tall
unblistered feet
grace new boots
slick with new dubbing

Protect well
pink skin
unused to exercise
and the outdoors

We are ready

As never ready

Let's go

Note: It is actually not so easy to know quite where to start the journey; as the Wall was not a stand-alone edifice but part of an interconnected system of roads, tracks, forts, towns, farms and peoples that, far from being static, was in a constant state of flux across both time and space. But **Ravenglass**, a natural harbour formed by the confluence of 3 rivers (the Esk, the Irt and the Mite) as they make their rendezvous with the sea seems like a good a place.

Ravenglass (Glannoventa)

The name of Roman Ravenglass is not certain it may have been Glannoventa (as I have guessed) or Tunnocelum. Whatever the case it today occupies a relatively quiet spot although a remnant of a Roman bath house can be seen still standing to a height of more than 3m.

We can only imagine the scenes, almost 1700-2000 years ago, when this was a bustling harbour; full of noise and colour, clashings and chatterings, arrivals and departures, trade and military; a supply base for Roman ships back and to from the wider Empire; up and down the Cumbrian Coast; garrisoned by troops from modern-day France.

The Fort initially of Turf and Timber then rebuilt in Stone, a Civil Settlement evolving alongside, a serious fire breaking out in the 300's

And not far North there stands the Neolithic Greycroft Stone circle, a reminder of the past that the Romans encountered (and did not destroy) — now in juxtaposition with a Nuclear Power Station.

We can already see how Time layers, swirls and eddies — we have taken our first step

John S. Langley

Red Dawn

There is a Red Dawn in the East
Blood red and full of foreboding
Vermillion creeping skywards
Bringing the sound of thunder
In a silence that is too deep

The omens are not good my friend
There has been fire seen in the sky
Dread in the reading of entrails
Birds flying North in the Winter
There is the smell of change in the air

We must arm
We must watch
and wait for this Dawn

to bring a new day
Or a new night

B 100 AD

John S. Langley

Safe Harbour

Out of the wind
Where the angry waves subside
the yellow torch lights ripple late
into the night

Safe haven for
foreign sail in strange waters
arriving now for the first time
strong and anxious

There is no turning back

80-100 AD

When

When the invaders came with catapults
And arrows, and sharp swords
They found ruins as old to them
as they to us

Like us
They were the Present Once

40-100 AD

Moresby (*Gabosentum*)

Think of it. They came from all points of the Roman compass; North from modern Germany, South from Morocco, East from Syria, West from Spain; from all four corners of the Roman world to join the cultural, lingual, military, melting pot that was the Wall socio-economic community.

The Roman cause brought mobility with it and as we step though our journey I will attempt to point out where at least some of the people who made part of their lives here originated from — using modern-day Country names for ease.

Moresby Roman Fort, possibly named Gabrosentum, was occupied by infantry from Italy, Eastern France, Bulgaria and inevitably attracted an associated civilian settlement.

It is North of St Bees Head that towers 90m above the Sea and shrieks with the calls of kittiwakes, fulmars, guillemots, razorbills, cormorants, puffins, shags and herring gulls whilst the Black Ravens scavenge and the Peregrine Falcons prey. No Roman remains have been detected here but they must have stood windswept here, the water streaming down their cheeks.

Shadows on the Wall

John S. Langley

Moon and Clouds

The Full Moon holds sway
sets shadows in the grey
Unaware of the dark clouds
approaching

First the cloud edges
lit silver enhances
the scene as they creep across
the Moon's face

The shadows darken
the bright Moon slips from sight
And in the ensuing black
silence reigns

Only a glimmer
through the obscuring clouds
promises a faint return
of the light

Behind shading clouds
Rigantona meets with
Luna to argue it out
in private

Note: *Rigantona is a Celtic goddess of the Moon; Luna is a Roman goddess associated with the Moon (Diana is another)*

B 100 AD

Feelings on Arrival
(Never to be Spoken aloud)

Whose Shores are these
What Land
What Life

Who brought me here
across the stormy Sea
without a choice

No chance of turning back

For Now
For Ever

Fearful
But not Forsaken

Not yet

100'S AD

Burrow Walls (Magis)

I tend to think of the Roman period as a homogeneous whole but that cannot possibly have been the case; a Roman of the 380's AD would hardly have recognised his counterpart of the 80's AD – just as we would have difficulty relating to the people who lived in the early 1700's - scary isn't it.

There's not much known and not much left of Burrow Walls. Its prominent site, partly lost to erosion, lends itself to linkage with a chain of coastal signal stations.

The stone has been taken as a source of ready building materials (a common occurrence along the Wall system); buildings from Medieval times (400's - 1400's AD) now regularly in ruin themselves – the stone taken and used again (and again) in later constructions.

Shadows on the Wall

John S. Langley

Strangers

You look quite like me
But I can't understand a word
you say

You move quite like me
But I don't get your gesture's
meaning

I smile, you smile too
But I don't know if we're smiling
at the same thing

100's AD

Letter Home

Dear Mother
Thank you for your letter and parcel
I am quite well thank you
The weather here is quite similar
to our own in sweet Southern Italy
and everybody here is very nice

I hope my
youngest sister has now settled down
and is chasing after
just the one man and not several
She was getting quite a reputation
and is known by some people even here

My manful
regards to Father and please tell him
that I can now respect
his decision to send me to join
the Cavalry as I am beginning
to love horses and all that goes with them

John S. Langley

P.S Please
don't send food as it seems to suffer
from the long journey and
the smells are quite revolting, it took
us a week to get rid of them, but do
send more of those woollen socks and
leggings

Must go now
I'm being summoned
Your Loving Son
Always ....

Note: *In WW1 there were a lot of 'I'm fine'
letters written to anxious family back home
that were more reassuring than the reality of
the Trenches could have justified.*

100'S AD

gods

The gods are everywhere
In the waters
The trees
Earth
The very air we breathe

They hold my fate in their hands

I hope they hold it carefully

100'S AD

Maryport (Alavna Carvetiorvm)

On a prominent plateau (from where, on a good day, you can see the Isle of Man) Roman Maryport was well-connected to the road system and surrounded by a burgeoning civil settlement.

Troops from Italy, Austria, North Africa, Spain, Croatia are known to have been here along with Officers from Israel, Romania, Southern France.

This was a bustling area — Cavalry, Infantry, the nearby Harbour, paved streets, Industrial activity (metal working), Temples, Cemeteries (inc. the 'Serpent Stone')….

There is even a distinct possibility that the Emperor Hadrian himself paid a visit during his short time in Britannia — perhaps as he was cogitating on the building of a Wall (!?)

Shadows on the Wall

Snowdrops

Pushing up green through
such hard ground
braving harsh frosts
for what?

To be the first to
flower white
on a white Earth
in Spring

Or is it simply
in answer
to Nature's call
to act

Denied only on
pain of death
eternally
damned

We are like you
We don't know either

Every Spring

Power

Listening to you I remember that
you were useful to me
when you dealt with my enemies
But now that it's done
Do I still need your help?

As I talk with you I can see that
you don't understand that we
helped you because we needed an in
and now that we're here
we're not going anywhere

As I talk to you I wonder if
you are listening to me
or just smiling in that noxious way
My hope is that you will go soon
Now that your work is done

As I pretend to listen to you I know that
you will soon understand that we
have the power and are the masters
not the mercenary soldier
slaves you took us to be

Soon you will understand who is boss
But in the meantime keep talking
and I'll just smile and nod

100's AD

Beckfoot (Bibra)

Beckfoot is another piece in the Coastal jigsaw of Milecastles, Turrets and Watchtowers that would have provided the Romans a means of communication and control.

The Fort straddles the Roman road and there were Cavalry from Hungary here, granaries, bath house, cemeteries.

There was also a large Roman Fort at Kirkbride (unknown Latin name) timber and turf built before the Wall and never rebuilt in stone - so it's function may well have been superseded when the Fort at Bowness was built.

For these reasons and because there's nothing really to see today I've relegated it to this footnote - sorry !

Shadows on the Wall

Mistletoe

On the sixth night of the Moon
As the white horns wane

The mistletoe is neat cut
from the Oaken branch

Where it has appeared from air
A gift from the gods

And thanks are spilt in bull's blood
white as the Moon

Respectful ceremony
in Secret Groves

where an elixir is made
carefully at night

And if properly prepared,
Offerings properly accepted,
Instruction properly followed,
can bring health and fertility

neutralising all Earthly poisons

B 100 AD

Mizpah

May the LORD
Watch over
each of us

Whilst we are apart
from each other

I ask that
the One God ....

(The rest of the inscription is lost)

500's AD

John S. Langley

Bowness-on-Solway (Maia)

250 yards or so West of the Roman Fort at Bowness, looking North across the Solway Firth, the Wall both joined and emerged from the Water.

The Fort, initially of turf and timber, later rebuilt in stone, was large enough for a garrison 1,000 strong. With Legions from Italy, soldiers from Spain, a large civilian settlement to the South and evidence of Sea Trade this must have been an important base and centre of commerce.

It is a shame that at our 2000 years distance we only have a few roman-sided **written sources** whose accuracy we must ponder. With so long an exposure to Roman writing why didn't the local tribes learn to write things down!? It's like relying on a history only written by the Conservative Party - better than nothing but needing heavy doses of salt!
Can you imagine how much richer our heritage would be if we had at least some weighty narrative fragments of the 'Barbarian's' side of the story!

Shadows on the Wall

John S. Langley

Me, The Wall

It is said that it was
the Romans that birthed me
Tho I am of this land
My bones, veins, organs
are made from the stone,
the sod, furnace forged lime
eons in the building
for this end

Turf Wall and timber was
my infant state in some parts
before harder raw stone
My base was Broad then
Narrow as I rose
evolving, strengthening
through experience
and dieting

Labour, Design and Sweat
put me together in short
shrift to stand proud and be
seen for many a mile
A symbol of might
and of ability
No other Fathers could
I have had

Shadows on the Wall

Over the years I have
to admit that I've had one
or two makeovers a
nip here a tuck there
a full Service now
and again whilst changing
hands many times as
my time flew

There was even a time
when I was forlorn, these things
happen; and another
when my ancestry
was strangely questioned,
hotly disputed, but
I'm pleased to say that's
over now

John S. Langley

It's true that I have seen
better days, my height reduced
shabbily dishevelled
in appearance but
I have seldom been
as popular as I
am today; who would
have thought it

Funny
the way
things
turn out

Notes: *Wall - Best guess height 12ft,*
probably castellated with a Wall walk and
possibly rendered White. At least three
Roman Legions contributed to its construction
(although they would undoubtedly have had
lots of – underappreciated? - help).
Nowhere does original Wall still stand to its
original height .

TimeLine

Pax Romana?

Physical power alone solves no problems
secures no victories
What counts is the way power is used
With swagger and contempt
or with prudence
discipline
and magnanimity

What really counts the most is the purpose
to which the power
is applied whether for liberation
or to impose superiority
to have a giant's
strength
but not to use it

like a giant

Note: *With homage to JFK's speech Amherst,
October 26 1963 (The bit he didn't say) -
3 weeks before his assassination.*

100's AD

John S. Langley

Solway

Salt water washes clean
the sand
Heavy footprints disappear
in swirls
of in-rushing tides

A man of all ages,
of all places,
of all races,
or maybe it is a woman
- it does not matter -
watches

The sky shrieks
the cry of Gulls
to ears that see
to eyes that hear
and feels the salt breath
brush across exposed skin

Look again
There is no one there
There are no footprints

The Gulls cry

500's AD

First to Last

Boots are the most important thing
Being well-shod on these hard footings
The last thing you need are wet feet

Get good Boots, of the right size, wear
them in, soften the leather, tie them well
The last thing you need are blisters

From 122 to 2222
For as long as we are walking the Wall
The first thing you need are good Boots

2000's AD

John S. Langley

Drumburgh (Goggabata)

Here were troops from Eastern France brought to a part of the land were the building materials most easily attainable were turf and timber.

Then Red Cumbrian Sandstone was brought in to build and re-build; 250 million years in the making and from a Time that saw the largest mass extinction in the history of Life on our Planet.

And later — it would have been foolish to overlook such a convenient resource - buildings in the vicinity of the Wall, some of them quite substantial, rose on the Red Stone's back.

Whether this is 'destruction' or 'entrepreneurial spirit' is moot but what is for sure is that this process of recycling has caused the effect of the presence of the Wall to resonate down the centuries to the present day.

The whole line, the whole area would not be the same without it.

Shadows on the Wall

Curlew

Walking the Terra Firma
through these parts
where the bogs are deep
and treacherous

Easy to be led astray
by the unwary
though others thrive
on its bounty

Brown mottled bird with your
long curved beak
Why do you cry out
so plaintively

Are you spirit or messenger
Sent to warn us
Shades of ancestors
coursing through you

Your cries haunt my sleep
Flying in dreams
Low across sands I'll
never see again

100's AD

Eagles

High, high above
A far ranging
aerial view
Seeking prey
but not averse
to an easy meal
of carrion

Below grounded
men gathered round
a carved image
held up high
above carnage
to rally the troops
and look up to

100's AD

Birrus Britannicus

Pull tight the cloak
thick with lanolin
To keep out this blasted
cold

that wants to cut
razor edged scarring
sharp to the red marrow
bone

And the hood too
That keeps tempests from
troubling a hair on your
head

The quality
is good even if
you have to pay through the
nose

For it

Note: The **Birrus Britannicus** was a woollen hoody; thick, warm and largely waterproof. A speciality of Britain; hugely prized and bringing high prices.

100's AD

Your Wall Needs You

Come work the Land
We'll keep you safe
You and your loved ones
It will be the best thing
you've ever done

All we want is
to be kept fed
Morning, Noon and Night
3 meals a day is not
a lot to ask

Is it ?

100'S AD

Burgh by Sands (Aballava)

This was a Fort built for Cavalry that crossed the Wall. Troops came from Belgium, Holland and North Morocco and, as 'normal', a civilian settlement was spawned.

It was in this area that, 1,000 years later, in 1307, Edward I of England came to die.

Nicknamed "Longshanks" because of his height he was also said to be temperamental and intimidating; particularly in his brutality towards Scotland.

In 1307 Robert the Bruce was in re-ascendancy and Edward was determined to confront the threat. Unfortunately for Edward (but not for the Scots) he developed dysentery and on 7th July, having encamped at Burgh by Sands, he died.

There is a memorial close by, carefully protected by an iron fence.

Shadows on the Wall

John S. Langley

Vallum

Listen my friend, shovelling muck,
digging a regulation deep ditch
in stony ground,
ain't no fun

Look at me hands, all raw and cut
through piling heaps of dirt
on either side,
regulation high

And remembering to lay those
gated crossings, regular like,
across the whole,
nicely and neatly

Them men on the Wall, with their stone,
they can mark their stretch alright,
leaving good luck,
symbols carved deep

But what mark can we leave, for our
sweat and blood, in the service,
to remember,
who dug the Vallum

100's AD

Real Life I

Fluid that's what I'd call it
Count up the beds
How many can be housed?
If only you knew
the reality of things

It's more like a hostel
than a homestead
Go here, go there, each one
assigned to their work
if they're fit enough

Sick and injured wander
about looking quite
sorry for themselves but
there's no sympathy
to offer them here

with plenty of hard work
still to be done
using all our fine skills
Honed and adapted
over the passing years

John S. Langley

A Centurion will
check it all out
when there is one about
Whether we like it
or not His view is law

At least it's not boring
you never know
what's going to happen
one day to the next
That's one thing for sure

200's AD

A Turn of Events

Bad water
Such a simple thing
Can bring a Hammer to his knees
and change the course
of history

Good Luck
for the waiting Scots
To see an army stop and turn
and watch a body
taken back South

Not North
as was the last words
The heat of hatred quashed in death
as was never
lost in life

1300's AD

John S. Langley

Haaf Fishing

Line the mounted net
astride
the turning tide

Hold down to billow
seeking
the sleek silver

Salmon powering
in their
own element

Catch, raise, gaff the proud
fish and
hang from your belt

A fine catch netted
to feed
the onshore mouths

1400's AD

Shadows on the Wall

Note: *Haaf netting is a method of fishing for salmon on the Solway estuary. Thought to have been introduced by the Vikings. The net is mounted on a rectangular frame 18 feet long by 5 feet high and supported by three legs – the fishing is done at the turn of the tide.*

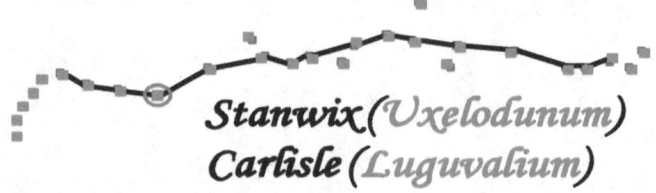

Stanwix (Uxelodunum)
Carlisle (Luguvalium)

For me Roman Stanwix (North of the River Eden) and Carlisle (South of the River Eden) were too interconnected to be separated.

Here co-habited the Roman Legions and Auxiliaries (Cavalry from France) and the capital of the local pro-Roman Carvetii tribe.

There is evidence of building, re-building over 300 years of Roman occupation and of a thriving commercial and manufacturing town with, to the South, repair shops for military equipment, glass, pottery and a Mansio (Inn) — even an Amphora 'Old Tangiers Tunney-fish relish of excellent, top quality' that contained fish sauce from Cadiz.

After the Romans left Carlisle changed hands several times in successive disputes between Scotland and England; that only began to calm down when the two Countries were United under a common King – James I/VI.

When St Cuthbert was shown the City in 685 he remarked on a 'marvellously constructed fountain of Roman workmanship'.

Shadows on the Wall

John S. Langley

Samhain

The Light is fading from the Day
Night and Dark and Cold are masters
for the coming time

The cattle are in from the pasture
culled for the feast and to match the store
of Winter fodder

Torch-lit gatherings surround fires
staving off the Dark, cleansing the year,
giving protection

from the Spirits and the Dead that
crowd the edge where glare gives way to
shimmering shadow

a boundary too easily crossed from
Light to Dark, Life to Death intertwining
bringing fear too close

Food and Drink is offered in set places
in welcome exchange, a small price to pay,
to curry favour

In the centre of the throng a fore-teller
warns of a greater darkness coming over water
her second sight roars

out the words, competing with the crackling
fury of the bonfires, as they drift away and across
the open boundary

into the Otherworld, stirring lost passions
lost amidst the feasting revelry in this World,
on this godless Night

Note: *The Celtic festival of Samhain was held on the night of 31st October (our Halloween) after the cattle had been brought down from their Summer pastures. A number were slaughtered for food/feasting and to match the supply of Winter fodder available. Special bonfires were lit, deemed to have protective and cleansing powers. It was a time when the boundary between this World and the Otherworld was weakened and could be easily crossed.*

B 100 AD

John S. Langley

Tideline

Astride the Tideline
Washed back and to in History
The turmoil of boundary changes

Built
Demolished
Deserted
Repaired
Besieged
Besieged
Besieged

The waves buffet the junction
between Rivers Eden, Caldew, Petteril
between Kings
between Lands
between Families
between friends

Buffeting the people
into an amalgam of uniqueness
Tempering them Strong, Stoic
Created in an undertow
from attempts to undermine

Not to be underestimated
Never
Ever

Shadows on the Wall

As a tide washes
Not away
but fresh
burying
hiding or
rolling smooth

Some taken on the surge
lost in the white water
the undulating waves
of perpetual movement

But still the place endures
and learns
to withstand the tides
with new ideas

That's what we do
the Old Man said
Sitting looking out
and thinking back

That's what we do
and we'll keep doing it

TimeLine

Fire

Vulcan
Do not bring us
fear and destruction
with your Power
but allow us to harness

your gifts
for warmth and light
To signal danger
a call for help
Or to forge our Arms to Rule

Vulcan
We ask this

Note: *Vulcan, Roman god of fire - that can be an enemy or a friend. The Blacksmith's Forge can be considered one of the prime Sources of Roman Power.*

200'S AD

Seasonal Blood-letting

The Days are getting longer
The noon hours warming

Whose lives will we take
in this Season
How much Blood will be
on my Hands
And how much of it
will be mine

New Heads to display
It is our way
To dissuade
others

Staring at dead eyes
Knowing that I
have only the
bad dreams

to worry about

This Summer

200's AD

Mary Queen of Scots

It was only for two months
after the cold welcome
She had been given
A Queen and a prisoner
making her Royal demands

But as we spoke I began
to understand the hard
time she'd had of it
The way her long awaited
Son had been taken from her

to be a two year old King
in her place and She, on
her walks outside with
her Ladies in the Spring Sun,
chattering, still able to smile

Then I came to respect
her resilient nature
and hope her cousin
consider with Royal grace
her repeated entreaties

Note: *Carlisle Provided a prison for Mary, Queen of Scots from 18 May to 13 July 1568. Francis Knollys was her reluctant custodian. She was never to be Free again and was beheaded at Fotheringhay Castle on 8th February 1587.*

1500's AD

Castlesteads (*Camboglanna*)

Other English names for the Fort are Cambeck Fort or Walton House Station and it lies uniquely off the Wall but within the vallum. Within the Fort there may have been a platform for a Roman Ballista (effectively the Roman canon) and troops garrisoned here came from Holland, France and Belgium.

Again there is evidence of a civilian settlement and stone from around this area was used in the construction of Lanercost Priory.

The Priory was founded in the 1100's. Being a religious centre did not prevent it from being embroiled in the conflict between England and Scotland. Edward I of England and Robert the Bruce and later David II of Scotland 'visited' with differing degrees of friendliness.

In later centuries the Priory was 'frequented' by raiding parties of Border Reivers from whom it had to be defended.

Today it is a great place to visit!

Shadows on the Wall

Lanercost

Birthed of the Wall, a Priory
But no place of peace
as the Scots and the English squabbled
spilling cheaper blood for centuries
Pock-marking the Sanctuary with
Chronicled shot

Then came a Debatable age
when strength of arms made
the Law and families feuded for
generations forgetting all cause
but nurturing their hate down the years
to fight about

Now the air wafts history through
ruins or listens
to the hymns as they rise to Heaven
whispering across the silent graves
The place a quiet haven now, with tea
and chocolate cake

The buttered fruit cream scones
To die for

1300- 2000's AD

Woods

These Woods are different at night
when creaking sounds are louder
and shiver the black air

The Wolves have sway in the Dark
The Bear and the stealthy Lynx
We become the hunted

Tho now as the Sun shines in blue
through green to forest floor
We raise our spears

Spur our horses
Let loose the dogs
and hunt for sport

1100's AD

John S. Langley

Honey Bees

It is a brave man gets too close
to the bees nest as they
buzz their egress and return
sitting on the step
passing messages

But honey is a fragrant prize
Golden flow, sweet to steal
and I have Virgil's instruction
in my ears and a
wager on my back

So I'll wet and smoke the entrance
of the Hive and gird up
mind and hands and face for the
anticipated
stinging mass attack

I'm as ready as I will ever be
Here goes ......

200's AD

Reivers

On short sturdy steeds they appear
silhouetted in the gathering gloom
torches alight and held high

The vendettas next chapter is about
to begin with barns burned to the ground
and cattle taken and life lost

They say these are the Debatable Lands
but there is no debate in the air tonight
only blood lust and vengeance

for a wrong that is to right a wrong
that no-one can now remember the truth
of and could not care less about

The blood is up, the Reivers night is nigh
The horses slaver against their bits and
hooves and flames begin to move

Musket and pistol are loaded with shot
A family waits in their Bastle to hear
the clattering of their fate

1500's AD

Banks Turret

The Turret was originally set in the turf wall which was later changed to stone and there is very clear evidence that the Turret was stone built prior to this change.

Inside the Turret are two possible hearths (allowing for a degree of creature comforts).

There are great views — to the South (!?) and at the top of the nearby rise to the East are the remains Pike Hill Signal Tower; its early construction and importance evidenced by the fact that the Wall itself was diverted to accommodate it — its facing angles allowing it to be part of a long distance signaling system.

Shadows on the Wall

John S. Langley

Turret Truth

A ladder gives access, two floors
and the ability to light
a signal flame
if need arises
or when lightning strikes

We look out from under cover
We built the Wall and you know
we're not stupid
We're not going to
stand in pouring rain

For no reason

200's AD

Note: There is doubt about the design of the Wall Turrets — in particular their upper storey and roof — I just can't believe the Romans wouldn't have provided themselves with the best protection from the elements they could.

There are lots of Turret remains to be seen along the route, for example Turret 33B, 35A between Housesteads and Carrawburgh.

I've chosen this one because of the views.

Birdoswald (Banna)

Built on a high promontory the position of the abutting Wall changed with function as the Fort had a Cavalry interlude before returning to Infantry duties. The Infantry came from Transylvania/Romania then Bulgaria and the Wall was first of Turf and Timber before being replaced by a 'Narrow Foundation' stone Wall. An extensive civil settlement grew up and Bath house, Cemetery, Altars attest to longevity

The site was occupied centuries after the Romans left and the presence of a large timber building (Hall) has been detected.

Antiquaries 'rediscovered' the site from 1500s (Reginald Bainbrigg) – 1800s and found such ruins, such evidence of a lost civilisation/time, that put them in awe.

The effect of seeing the remains for the first time must have been like discovering a Mayan Temple in the Mexican forest. The ruins, partially re-conquered by nature; walls climbing green, towns, streets, altars; the hand of the stonemason writ deep.....

Shadows on the Wall

Dinner Party

Please do come along
It wouldn't be a party
without you

Thank you for coming
I've got to say that you're
looking well

Did you see her hair
Wasn't it one of the most
awful sights

200's AD

Winter's Heroes

Sharp is the cold and hoar the frost
that lies on the land and sets the white hairs
rigid in the old man's beard

Ahead the gnarled oaken door shines
under and around and through with yellow
signaling firelight within

The watchman waits and asks and goes
and returns with welcome Winter greetings
to enter and sit and eat

with thanks the old man does as bid
and warms and eats and answers soberly
the slurred queries from young men

John S. Langley

Their brown beards beer soaked, their clothes of
wolf and wool, their heads unsteady from the
long feasting and deep drink,

Mostly from the drink, thick, hoppy,
frothy, healthy in a moderation
surpassed many hours ago

Then the Master of the Hall asks
the old man to take a place by the fire
so that all can hear and see

his bleached white hair, his scorching
pock-marked skin, wise eyes rheumy in the glow
glittering under tangled brows

Shadows on the Wall

And he, older still than his years,
begins to chant loud and full of gusto
from memories recovered

of battles won, of times long past
of times both real and mythic, of tales of
beasts and heroes intertwined

As truth and lies are intertwined
to suit the ear of the cheering, churring,
raucous men and the moment

And into the Night the Bard sings
and answers calls for known and lost tales
for new ventures and new words

John S. Langley

that hold fast the Hall until his voice
drops and in somnolent husky tone he tells
of life and death and sleep and

valour and unforgotten names,
reverent, head-healing, reassuring,
as hope-filling words bringing

full meaning to all and purpose
to the future as the noise begins to
subside the fire collapses

and embers dart with yellow tongues
The tangle bearded man gratefully takes
the proffered payment in hand

Shadows on the Wall

tucks food away, the grease oozing
grasping fingers and slips away past night
watchers and steps out once more

into the breath fogged dark, bathed silver
by the Moon, and trudges deep set footprints
that will be gone by morning

Inside salving sleep overwhelms
the winter heroes, dogs chew discarded
scraps of bone and tear sinew

and a few wide eyed children hide in
the shadows chewing over what they have heard
and seen, grinning to each other

900's AD

John S. Langley

Stones I

Look closely
Each stone is a country
Made up of warring colonies
of lichen and moss

Symbiosis
A fungi, algae and
cyanobacteria partnership
creeping slowly forward

in annular
advance and sharing
structure and sustenance and growth
of tenths of a millimetre

a year in
such hostile terrain
with time on their side and little
regard for right angles

2000's AD

Brown Trout

Hic, hic, mea est
Here let my numb fingers
Slip under
through the cold river's water

Come here my beauty
Golden bellied
mottle spotted
silver scaled sleekness

I anticipate the reverence
with which your grilled flesh
Will fill our
empty stomachs

Hic, hic
Come
Come here
My beauty

Let my fingers caress

My loving hands await

Note: *I've never tickled a Trout but I love the idea. The Greek writer Oppian refers to it in the 100's AD and Aelian in the 200's AD so it is a technique that could have been known to some of the Romans/Auxiliaries in Britain.*

200's AD

Fanum Cocidi

The Latin place name is after a Romano-British god Cocidius; the only place in the North with this form of naming. Manned by Infantry probably from Transylvania/ Romania and Belgium the Fort was twice destroyed and rebuilt before being abandoned in the later 300s.

The magnificent Bewcastle Cross dates from the 600s and has runic inscriptions.

There are also the ruins of Bewcastle Castle which was built from Roman stone around 1092, destroyed in 1173, rebuilt towards the end of the 1300s, fell into decay by the early 1400s, repaired, then destroyed in 1641 with much of the stone later removed and reused in the construction of nearby buildings.

An example of the layers of turbulence that Time plays over a single site — although there were extended periods of relative calm in between.

Shadows on the Wall

Bewcastle Cross

Knotted decoration
intertwined animal design
Four faces of stone
Runic inscriptions
Memorialising
and praying for prayer
For sins
For souls

700's AD

Jeopardy

I love you like a brother
Better than a brother
and would trust you
with my life

But not with my women and
not at the gaming board
I know you well
I'm not daft

It is sad to admit when
Love is not as strong
On both sides
In both directions

That's Life I guess
You can't always
get back what
you hope you gave

300's AD

Carvoran (Magna)

Carvoran Fort is not only South of the Wall it is South of the Vallum as well. It was manned by Infantry from Croatia and Archers from Syria. It again attracted civilian settlement to its walls – which is so commonplace that such an arrangement can only have been to mutual benefit.

Out of the 300 years or so that the Romans were around I would like to believe that there were more years of peace than of war and that when hostilities did break out they were more sporadic and localised than total or universal - if this wasn't the case I think the Romans would have expired of exhaustion well before they were finally called away.

Thirlwall and Blenkinsopp Castles are also in this area – their later construction benefiting from Roman stone.

Shadows on the Wall

John S. Langley

Scars on the Land

Dug deep with iron edges
forged in flame and swung
with sweat and muscle to
fulfil a purpose

Scraping at the surface
to shape a scar face
of lines where control
can be controlled

Scars dug deep enough
for healing so slow that
2000 years is not enough
to wipe them away

They made their mark
The scar-makers
They left but left their mark
We can still see them

What marks will we leave
We scar-makers
For others to find
In 2000 years

100'S AD

Settling

And the months pass
and the weeks
the days

I've begun to forget what
I always promised
to remember

This is where I am now
For good or for bad
I'm accepting

Expecting nothing more
Nothing less
Come here you

You make the difference

300's AD

Recycling

Here was the sturdy Wall threw down
Here was the might of Rome mastered
the very stones ripped from their place
remodelled to Home and Bastle

A strongpoint for raids and retreat
when Laws were made unto themselves
A new might was right in the land
and Murders no less than before

Now the ruined stone stands all bereft
for the Mighty to look upon
and see the Land that lies around
is farmed in these more peaceful times

Note: *Close to where the Wall was `thirled', or thrown down, are the ruins of Thirlwall Castle. Constructed of Wall stone it was itself reused for farm buildings in later times. Bastle is one of the names for a Border Reiver Fortified House*

300-1800 AD

Regrets

Here is my Chest of Gold
Here where I buried it
misguided
in this shallow grave

Take it I beg of you
and tell me where He lies
He who I
wrongly mistrusted

Drove away and cannot
find though I now beseech
that He come
back into my arms

Note: *A Lord Blenkinsopp married a rich Lady who worried he had only married her for her money. So she secretly buried her treasure in the Castle grounds. His Lordship was so distressed he left never to be seen again. The Lady later regretted her actions but it was too late and she died lonely and remorseful - although her ghost may still be seen!*

1400's AD

Great Chesters (Aesica)

The Fort is attached to the Wall on its North side and guards Caw Gap where the burn passes through the line of the wall. Infantry from Belgium, Switzerland and North West Spain were present here and the Headquarters Building houses an underground Strongroom (not uncommon).

The way plans evolved and changed is demonstrated here as the Fort is built over the position of Milecastle 43 and the original 'Broad Wall' intent (foundations) was superseded by 'Narrow Wall' construction. The Military Way runs through the West to East Gates and Bath house and civil settlement are evident.

One important point is that Water is supplied to the Fort by an Aqueduct that runs for 6-7 miles through the (hostile?) land on the North side of the Wall and past non-Roman homesteads — questioning our understanding of the Wall as Border and the relationships that existed between 'civilised conqueror' and 'subdued barbarian'.

Shadows on the Wall

John S. Langley

Water

Life Blood aplenty streaming clean
to drink or wash or flush
an essential element
without which
the desert would not sustain
all of these people
There would be
no Wall
And a whole different Story

Tutored water flows a winding
6 miles from the North side
to save a half mile carry
from Burn side
to the heart of the Great Fort
Who would run such a
precious thing
exposed
through enemy territory?

Damn clever these Romans

200's AD

Windhover

Dynamic stability against the wind
Effortlessly maintained
with twisting body and
ruffled feathers

Black eyes searching the green
For rustling movement
of careless fur and tail
Patience patient

Heedless of all else than her own
ambition to feed young
waiting cowering low
Impatient hunger

Above
Waves of grass
Into the sea of green

TimeLess

Hard Frost

It was a Hard Frost we had
Crunching forward through sharp fields
blades breaking underfoot
like shards of glass

An untamed land subdued
in an embrace held ice fast
for a time in a time
only slumbering

The Winter Sun blinding our
eyes so that we could not see
into the future nor
past memory

It was a Hard untamed Frost
sending shivers through old bones
to touch the not yet born
to the marrow

200's AD

Night Watch

Cramped with cold
Blue as the painted people
The stars bright in insolence
The Moon white like the snow
Shining ice crystals cover my cloak
and sparkle like mocking eyes
revelling in discomfort

In the silence
you can hear the snow melt
Ticking, crackling, cracking
like dry frozen bones
From this height you can see firelight
dotted across the land a yellow
warmth I cannot feel

I curse the dice
that made fool of me and lost
the woollen cloak I bought
my Birrus Britannicus
worth a month's wages and more
in this cold where I now stamp my feet
and swear up to the gods

200'S AD

John S. Langley

Under Attack

I.

We've got Moles
undermining the walls
Big Brown Rats
sleek and sneaky
that look better fed than we are

The Foxes
are so cheeky slipping
in to fight
with the birds for
our discarded bloody offal

The Badgers
are much more skittery
Wolves and Bears
with no respect
for our mastery of the world

Mites, midges,
Hook worm, Round worm, scabies
Snakes with the
v of a viper
impressed on their poisonous head

Shadows on the Wall

The vapours
bringing disease from the
reeking swamps
stinking of death
You have to watch your every step

II.

We're under
attack from head to toe
Inside and
outside and from
every quarter under the Sun

Cut off my hair
Down to the scalp
and burn it

Boil my clothes
For as long as
it will take

Scrub my skin with
oils and ointments
I will pay
This damn itching
these festering Lice
will kill me

If I don't get them first !

200's AD

John S. Langley

Chesterholm (Vindolanda)

Here were Legionaries, Cavalry, Infantry from Belgium and France, an extensive civil settlement, livestock, shops and industrial premises. Two bath houses are evident and the extensive archaeology carried out here has uncovered complex phases of building, rebuilding, destruction and over-building.

This is a place where (under professional supervision) we were allowed to pay to get down on our knees in the mud and scrape gently away at the layers of history for a few days; unearthing shards of pottery, sheep bones and a Roman coin – a privilege and a pleasure!

In the Museum can be seen the benefits of waterlogged ground – the survival of fragile leather items, textiles and, of course, those writing tablets – quite remarkable!

Shadows on the Wall

Wolves

Howling at the Moon
They awaken the night
with their calling

Hunting in the Day
together in Packs
for added strength

Loyal to the Cause
they take our sheep
to feed themselves

Alone in the Woods
We fear thee more
than any other

Relentless in the chase
We hunt thee not
for any food

Shadows on the Wall

But as an equal
To be subdued
Pax Lupus

And to wear your skins
and teeth with
deep respect

This is our way
we know no other
to be top dog

100's AD

John S. Langley

Beer

As I sit here hammering nails
making shoes
I can smell the beer brewing
next door

In my mind's eye I see clearly
the rich froth
foaming, bubbling and bursting
next door

I'm looking forward to tonight
a good drink
oysters and swapping stories
next door

200's AD

Messaging

I.

The hand that holds the stylus
bids you come
and quickly

I cannot write more or clearly
Too many eyes
Conspire near

Believe me when I .....

II.

Write this, write that
To Mother, Lover, Friend
Do it now, now, now
I'll never be short of work

That is for sure
though my old fingers ache
around the stylus
and my head around the words

As long as my
sight holds and my mental
strength ....

The line was left unfinished

200's AD

Husband's Offering

I call on all you Nixae,
goddesses of Birth,
to give your Divine Protection
to my dear wife
who precariously carries
in her womb
our first child

Keep her womb in its right place
and let it not hold
on during her Birthing Labours
As Guardians
of Life's threshold open our child's
mouth to cry
it's first breath

Vagitanus hear my prayer
and Lucina who
brings children safely into light
read my scratched words
folded tight on Lead and placed
before you
Earnestly

200's AD

Real Life II

There's Birth and Death
Injury, Sickness
Family
Friendship
All here, all here

The Good and Bad
Mixture of Lawyers
Accountants
And the
Politicians

The strong Blacksmiths
Jewellers, Potters,
Stone Masons
Writers
Actors, Painters ....

Yes, we're all here
Too long a list
Too complex
To hand-
le in a poem

200's AD

John S. Langley

The Dig

On padded knees
from all corners
Scraping away the layers
Of time
Of soil
In the rain

Turf by the wheelbarrow
piled in new mounds
of no function

Then a find
A piece of pot rim
Black
Thick

Another fragment
terracotta
Thin
Signs of a pattern

Shadows on the Wall

Re-emerging into the light
Discarded then
treasured now
A makers mark

Sandwiches, tea
Exchanging news
then back to worn knees

Padded
In the rain
Hands cold in
mud splattered gloves

Happily paying for all
To hunt for treasure

1900's AD

Milecastle 37

Apparently built by the 2nd Legion and showing evidence of internal barracks and ovens, store houses and maybe even stables for a guessed compliment of 10-20 men.

It seems to me there were some important aspects to Roman life and one of them was Rules – first that there were Rules, second that 'everybody' knew the Rules, third that it was clear that not following the Rules was a painful mistake and fourth that 'everybody' followed the same Rules.

The life of a Roman soldier, whether Roman citizen or not, whether infantry, cavalry or sailor, seems to have been Ruled by Rules – it may be hard, harsh or unforgiving but it had the benefit of being clear. Obey the Rules and you get money, food, clothing, shelter, chances of promotion and the promise of a comfortable dotage; disobey and all bets are off.
When life was short and choices stark this doesn't seem such a bad one.

Shadows on the Wall

John S. Langley

On Duty

Routes up to, down from
Back and fro through the Wall
No Centurion looking on
not a bad gig

Gates, Roads, North and South
bridging the deep ditches
and beds, a warm hearth, food and drink
helps the time pass

High walls keep out wind
the rain patters tiled roofs
There are a lot of worse places
to spend the night

100's AD

Note: I chose this Milecastle because of its position and its association to my own personal memories. There are lots of great Milecastles to see along the way — Poltross Burn (48), Cawfields (42), and Castle Nick (39) to name but a few.

John S. Langley

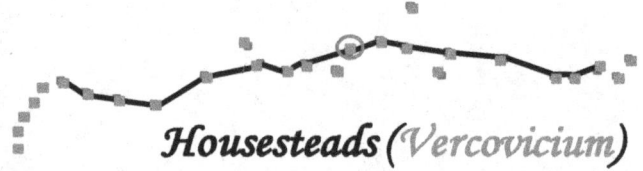

Housesteads (Vercovicium)

WOW! I'm completely biased because Housesteads is the first Wall Fort I can remember visiting - many years ago now. My favourite thing was then and still is the Latrine (I know it's sad isn't it). It's the cleverness of the design, the engineering, the hydraulics. And the more I learn the better it gets. The rock the Fort is built on is too hard for a well, the lie of the land too high for an aqueduct, so the water is got from the sky; collecting rainwater from the roofs, keeping it fresh through movement. And there was always the nearby Knag Burn where containers and mules could augment supplies.

I quite like the 'Murder House' as well!

The Fort (Latin name has a degree of uncertainty) was garrisoned by Infantry from Belgium, irregulars from Holland. The civilian settlement spread out from the Fort walls in all directions South, East and West and there is evidence of some extended periods of peace (and prosperity). However there is also evidence that the Fort was destroyed three times and of a final, sudden, destruction and desertion in the 400s.

The site was part-occupied by Border Reivers (Armstrongs) in the 1600's which may have had the unintended consequence of assisting its preservation.

Shadows on the Wall

John S. Langley

Whin Sill

The serpent Wall slithers silence
across the land
Laying straighter lines than Nature
thought fit to build

Stone scales unceremoniously scrape
foolish knuckles
Cracked whinstone from Whin Sill
Scar iron and leak sweat

Frozen snake whose back is broken
Too much to hold
back a tide of perpetual change
For too long

200's AD

Cold on the Wall

Iron men of Rome
wrapped thickly with wool and woven cloth
Stamping their feet and
grumbling over their braziers

Conquerors of Europe
patrols rocked by the freezing icy gusts
of winds from the North
harbinger of trouble

Followers of Mithras
wiping the rain from their rusting chain mail
thinking of another home of
missed warmth and wine

A passing phase of
enforced invaders for a century or four
engineering to leave their mark
whilst battling against the cold

200's AD

John S. Langley

Collecting Debts

It's a hard thing
The Wall

Hard men
Hard times
Hard frosts

Harsh conditions
Breeding discontent
Looking after No.1

First
Last
Always

That's all I'm doing
Don't blame me
Blame the Wall

You lost the game
Now pay the piper
Or face the consequences

At home
In work
Everywhere

So empty your purse
Let's see what you've got
For now

200's AD

Outside the Gates

I.

Blacksmith, Cobbler, Bath House
Baker, Carpenter, Market Stall

Money Lender, Fishmonger
& Entertainment for the troops

Women, Wives and Children
Kept close but not too close

The Fort is less disciplined
outside the thick wooden gates

But there are still rules to play by
and business to be done

II.

What can't be done inside the Fort
We do outside
On the doorstep
So there's not far to go
For essentials
Happily interdependent
Inside and out
Placing orders
Manufacturing goods
We've got it sussed

200's AD

John S. Langley

Skin Deep

There are no bodies left unmarked
The canvas skin born
to paint a life on

The days are hard and the iron edge
harder and sharper
as we cut and heal

To become who we are by chance
of birth, time and place
as if it were meant

The soldier's scars from sword the farmer's
from plough and hammer
dig in as deeply

Their minds honed, filled with who they are
and scarred by learning
as they go along

Are we as they, Are they as we
They are so different
We are so different

And yet the same?

300's AD

A Night at Twice Brewed

The boiling Bread pudding bubbled
full of flavour
giving off steam
Mingling in the smoke filled room

The men with their long white curved pipes
chewing the fat
after the beef
and potatoes all washed down

with unwatered strong beer the foam
smacking their lips
raucous amongst
stories of fat customers

silly but paying the full fare
Putting the food
on their table
and drink in their open mouths

John S. Langley

After a hard dry day's walking
trying to halt
the destruction
the removal of old stone

A ready source for farm buildings
Not knowing what
a difference
he'd made as he bathed in warmth

Enjoying the company
and a Brandy
to help him
to sleep

1800's AD

Note: ***William Hutton*** *was quite a chap. In 1801 at the age of 78 he walked 600 miles, including the 'entire length of the Wall', and wrote a book about it. On part of his journey he saw stone being taken from the Wall and remonstrated with the men for carrying out such wanton destruction – Good on him!*

Carrawburgh (Brocolitia)

The Fort lies on the Wall and was built over the Vallum. Infantry from SW France, NW Germany and Holland are evidenced as is the Bath House and civilian settlement.

Outside of the Fort lies the evocative Coventina's Well; built over a natural spring in reverence to the mysterious appearance of water from Earth (and the goddess Coventina) in both pre-Roman and Roman times. The near choking of the spring with goods and offerings was then a cause for surprise, delight, robbery, study and display in the 1800's. It is now difficult to locate overgrown and swamped in neglect.

Also here is the remains of a Temple to Mithras (examples are found in several places along the Wall). Mithras the Bull-Slayer with his connection to the Sun, Moon and Heavens his underground temples, torch lit and brightly painted, and the ranks, rituals, and rites associated with his cult must have been an attractive (and familiar) proposition for Wall Soldiers.

Finally, a little East of the fort is Limestone corner where you can see the point at which the Romans stopped battling to break the local stone to create a ditch and retreated; presumably to more productive work.

Shadows on the Wall

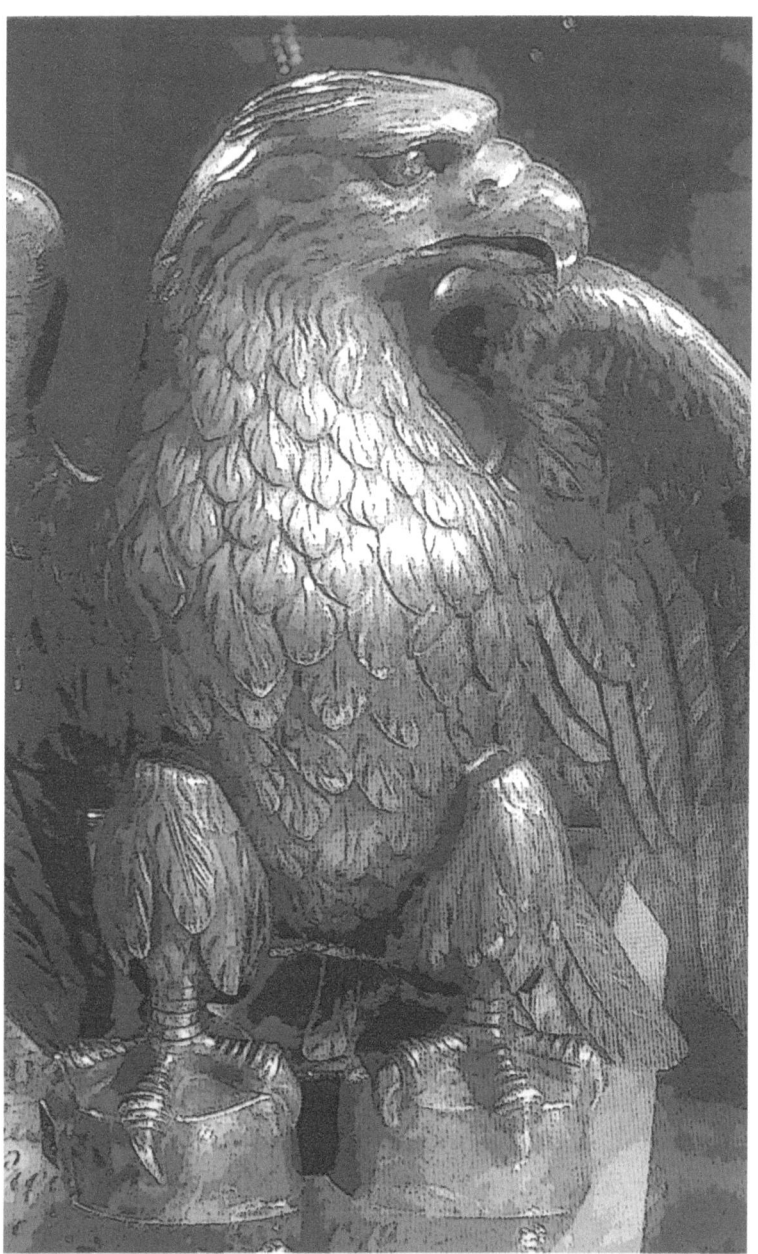

John S. Langley

Stones II

Stone hard as the Roman way
Not formed in regular shape
but forced to conform
by hammer and chisel
sparks flying in defence
but to no avail

Forced into right angles
Formed into rectangles
Carried as blocks

Wall built against the landscape
How the Roman surveyors
loved their straight lines
Taking no quarter of rivers
valleys or hills to build
as the crow flies

Packed cores of concrete
Vertical faces at 90 degrees
Built as they please

Note: *But they did not always succeed – abandoned half-worked stone at Limestone Corner gives testimony.*

100's AD

Military Zone

Vallum to Wall
A zone
Under control

Sheep, cows, horses
Keeping
the sparse grass down

For fast movement
A road
Keeps us mobile

Seen from the South
deep ditch
a Barrier

Easy defence
too hard
to overrun

Even if anyone
wanted to

300's AD

John S. Langley

Altar

I have a debt to pay
and coin in my hand

Prepare me an Altar
carved deep
in the hard stone

Carve the god's name
Invincible and Sacred
Add my name
My position
My Cohort
V S L M
Willingly and Deservedly
I Fulfilled
this Vow

300's AD

Different Outcomes

Always said these Incomers were full of crap
Working down in the drains
Under the latrines
I can vouch for it
You need a big shovel
And strong shoulders
To shift this lot

At least you'll be warm, they said laughing
Feeding the furnaces
Stoking the Bath's fires
I can vouch for it
The flames scorch my skin
I sweat in rivers
Keeping this hot

John S. Langley

Thank the gods I was forced to learn to write
Scratching out messages
Full of insignificancies
I can vouch for it
If you smile all the while
You get plenty of
Food from their pot

From far to be marketed like a lump of bread
I could not hide my spirit
But my Luck was with me
I can vouch for it
I married my Purchaser
And watch our first child
Asleep in her cot

300's AD

Coventina's Well

So many coins hid amidst my bubbling
waters I, Coventina goddess of this spring
Demand no more offerings
I am gorged with them

'Freely and deservedly' given
Inscribed and sculpted stones,
Silver, Bronze, Gold, Lead
Leather, Glass, Pottery,
Jet, Shale and Bone
The cranium of a human skull

And so many coins that
they cannot be counted but lifted
some stolen overnight
others melted down, bronze
and reformed into an Eagle

John S. Langley

An Eagle !
From a goddess of wells

Ignored for millennia
Adored by many

Walled and worshipped
Gorged with offerings

Abandoned for centuries
Rediscovered by accident

Shadows on the Wall

Stolen from by scholars
and blaggards both

Empty and unkempt
Left bereft

What next
I gurgle into the grass

I can wait
I am waiting

1800's AD

John S. Langley

(Walwick) Chesters (Cilurnum)

The Fort was built for Cavalry and spans the Wall; the main North, West and East Gates being on the North side of the Wall (similar to the Forts at Rudchester and Benwell).

There can be no coincidence that the site lies alongside the Bridge over the North Tyne; if you've got a potential weak point it seems sensible to put some troops alongside it to deter any 'misbehaviour'.

The Cavalry included troops from NW Spain, there are the remains of an underground Strongroom in the Headquarters Building, an associated civil settlement and the Bath House on the banks of the river is one of the highlights – you can almost hear the splashing, feel the sweating steam, the dry heat, the icy chill of the plunge. Here was a place for relaxation and recreation – as long as you didn't spare a thought for the guys stoking the fires.

John Clayton is to be thanked here as from 1834 he bought up Wall land to ensure its preservation – Thank You Mr. Clayton!

Eastwards From Chesters is Planetrees where the change of plan for 'Broad' to 'Narrow' Wall is evident and further still the site of the Battle of Heavenfield (633AD).

Shadows on the Wall

John S. Langley

Foundations

The stone Wall foundation
we have at our feet
can touch with our fingers
is about two metres wide
at this point

Further along you will see
the broad foundation
It is about three metres wide
and in some places
the narrow wall
has been built upon it

Questions ?

Did they change their minds?
They must have done

Why?
Who made the decision?
Did they have callouses on their hands
from lifting the stones?
How big were they ?
What were their names?
Did they enjoy what they did?
Could they sing as they worked?
How many were there?

Let's stick to what we know shall we

The stone Wall foundation is about
three metres wide
at this point ....

2000's AD

Strongroom

Protection piled upon protection
Locked Underground
The chests heave in the dark
Breathing full with Gold, Silver and Bronze

Inside the Headquarters stone Building
Guarded thrice over
The Cohorts Standards near
If anyone dare rob they steal from all

Keys upon keys to hard wrought iron locks
safely held in trust
Beware any that approach
Your reason must be as sound as the

Stone of my Walls
Of my deep flagged Floors
The thick wood of my Door
The metal of my Locks
The mettle of my Guards

Beware
Think hard before
you dare to
venture close

I hold treasure but
I hold death too

200's AD

John S. Langley

Central Heating

Under floor and
piped through walls
Hot air moved
by convection
Heat transferred
by conduction
Radiated to warm
pampered skins

Out of the rain

300's AD

Human vs Machine

Is this what it is like to be human
To stand all alone and feel comfort
in the presence of a far horizon
the deep Red
of the setting Sun

In Battle we function like a machine
As individuals we are dead
We are a collective an ordered swarm
Discipline
instead of feeling

Any incompetencies overcome
by the execution of routines
Making it far easier to obey
no matter
what the consequences

Sunsets forgotten

300'S AD

John S. Langley

Heavenfield

A cross out of place marks a cross
in space where prayers were offered
before, after or during as legend demands
in the lost histories of the victors

Oswald outnumbered but with God
on his side and the Wall protecting
his other fights for a kingdom newly acquired
against ill-prepared and over-confidence

Harsh is the chase to the Devil's Brook
and beyond a routed horde put to sword
edge accepting no parley or plea for mercy
A blood-letting to be turned into Song

A turning point for the righteous
Words let and lost in the heated air of the Halls
Not enough pens lifted for future clarity
Leaving us to speculate but not know

What actually happened here

600'S AD

Let slip the Dogs

The dogs have taken
a fine scent

Baying and straining
on their leash

Fox or Deer flushed
from their lair

The chase is on
let slip the dogs

1200's AD

High Rochester (Bremenium)

The furthest North our journey takes us. There must have been times when being here made you feel very exposed and the relative safety of the Wall a very long way away.

Keeping the garrison fed would have been a logistics issue with 'trouble' on the doorstep.

The Fort was built for Infantry and there is evidence of troops from Eastern France, Croatia, NE Spain.

The large number of internal Fort buildings with 'central heating' tells something about the conditions.

The walls of the Fort are thickened on the North and West sides and there are platforms for firing small ballista (onagri) giving protection to passage along nearby Dere Street.

Shadows on the Wall

John S. Langley

Loads of Loaves

Seven Thousand loaves a week
to feed a Legion
of up to Five Thousand men

Sounds a lot but it's less than
one and half loaves each
in a potato-free world

But a Fort may only have held
say 500 men
700 loaves a week

100 a day about
10 each working hour
Or one every six minutes

It must have been a tough job
Not good for someone
who wants in a social life

Manual, hot work, kneading
lots of ovens then
there's the butter and the cheese

Note: *They would have to wait 1200 years for the potato – arriving from Virginia, brought here by the colonists who were sent there in 1584 by Sir Walter Raleigh.*

300's AD

Picts

Your rigid love of straight lines
is ludicrous when it is far easier
to follow the land
It makes us laugh

Buildings with corners where
shadows lie deep and unsafe
When the circle
is the better way

You have no single thought that
is not told you in your camps
Discipline beyond
our temperament

Come let's be friends, we have
battled enough, we can wait
We can wait until
you've had enough

300's AD

John S. Langley

Crows

Anxious about my fate as
dawn breaks I see you perched
a silhouette

The black birds are gathering
sensing an orgy of blood
to feast upon

They settle on rock and branch
their black eyes glistening
their caw-caw

calls filling the silence of
pre-battle nerves before
the gory fight

Shadows on the Wall

A Murder clustered I feel
your cast iron confidence
of Victory

That whatever the day brings
Your belly will be full
by the end of it

300's AD

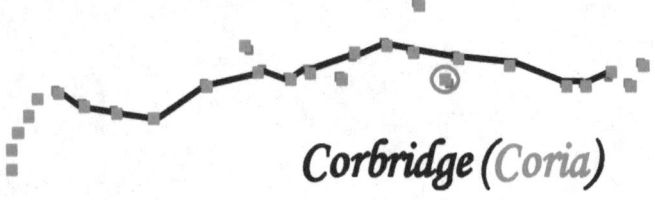

Corbridge (Coria)

South of the Wall and on Dere Street Corbridge gives good testament to 'what a difference a Wall makes'.

A Fort, with the Legions in evidence; a Town with evidence of wealthy merchants, craftsmen, silversmiths, jewelry-making (including trade with the peoples North of the Wall). The centre of an agricultural and mining (coal, lead and iron) area; supplied with water from an aqueduct, houses, granaries, shops, workshops, storehouses, fountains, temples, a bridge over the River Tyne to the South.

Bright colours, smells, sounds, an Inn for travelers (Mansio) – this must have been the place to be for a good night out!

Building and re-building, timber, turf, stone no wonder it all lasted into the 600's – even in 1201 King John ordered a search for treasure here – but apparently didn't find any.

Shadows on the Wall

John S. Langley

Wanderer

You have won the lottery of life
The Wanderer told me
in the Tavern last night
after I'd bought him another drink

You Romans are the Master Race
I think is what he said
Though his accent was strong and
his speech was slurred in the candlelight

You should bless your Luck and thank the gods
Were his very last words
As I lifted the sword to do my duty
and cut him as a Spy from this life

into the next

To return as a Roman?

Something to think on
I can still see his face

But I'm due on Duty
so maybe now
Is not the best time

300's AD

Blacksmith

The Hammer rises and falls
sending sparks scattering
Forging a blade of iron
turning, hissing its temper
through water and flame
repeatedly

Here is the Roman secret
Here is the beating heart
of Empire formed in the heat
for cool heads to rely on
Life and death are held
Sharp metal deep

300's AD

John S. Langley

Entertainment I

Let the games begin !
My denarii are on the big guy
painted Blue and wielding the axe
see his rippling skin

Yahoo! Wayyyyyy!
See how he snarls and swings his blade
no-one can get near enough to cut
at him as he strikes

Oooooh! Aaaaaaaah!
Cry foul! Taking him from behind
like that now look his blood gushing
onto the arena floor

Gaaaaaaa! Boooooo!
My money's down the drain, take him
away drag him out throw his body
to the rabid dogs

Bring on the next bout quickly !
I need to win my money back,
I've learnt my lesson - 10 coins on
the guy with the net !

Note: *My conjecture is that any 'civilised' Roman Town would have had an Arena as there was nothing the Romans liked better than a little bit of blood-letting in the name of Entertainment!*

300's AD

Snipping

The man brought me nicks and shavings
of Gold and Silver
And bade me craft a ring
Quickly

He was a brothel keeper and
I did not ask
only melted the metal
Pieces

I saw a woman wearing the
ring in the street
and only hoped that she
liked it

300's AD

John S. Langley

Ketchup

Granted it doesn't sound all that tasty
Crushed innards of fish
Eel, Mackerel
Soaked in heavily salted water
and left to ferment
for weeks

Pushed to the outskirts of habitation
Because of the smells
Filtered and sieved
Strained, bottled and flavoured with strong herbs
Mint, coriander
it works

Need to add taste to otherwise bland food?
This is the greatest
way to do it
Added to my own Mother's Lamb Stew
for example it's to
die for

Note: *Garum was a popular Roman fish sauce condiment – the Roman 'Tomato Sauce'.*

300's AD

Market Day

Bustling rustling push and pull
Bartering arguing towards a deal
Milling in gossip around the Bread
Gasping grasping beer-fuelled lust

Bashing crashing dashing people
Meshing messing pressing crowds
Men, woman, boys, girls, babes in arms
All sizes, colours, mixing together

Dawn till dusk meeting greeting
Fleeting chatter noisy secrets shared
Flirting touches quick in quiet corners
Promises promissory patter on parting

Walking home in knots
Planning for next time
Until next time
Can do better next time

Can't wait....

300's AD

John S. Langley

The Veteran

See this scar
This scratch?
That is deeper than it looks
and more severe

I got this scar in Gaul
A present from a charioteer
Pass me the wine
not the cheap one
and I'll tell you
the story
Of how I made him pay

See my pronounced limp
Not always?
It is worse than
it looks

I got this limp in Scotia
Care of a painted warrior
Buy me a calda
hot water and spiced
and I'll tell you
the story
Of how I took him down

Shadows on the Wall

Look here at my naked back
These light marks?
Are from nature's
sharp claws

These marks I got on a hunt
From a giant black bear
I will take posca
vinegar diluted to taste
and I'll tell you
the story
Of how I overcame the beast

Beer !
You offer me beer!

I am a Roman
Do you take me for a barbarian ?

Get out of here

Let others have the honour
Of hearing of my instructive life

300's AD

John S. Langley

Entertainment II

These old Greek tragedies bore me
Men wearing silly masks and
pretending to be women

I'll laugh and cheer with the rest though
trying to catch the eye of
that rich matron over there

Shadows on the Wall

She looks a little lonely and
I need a patron to help
me get up the social scale

She's glancing my way, she's smiling
I return her smile in spades
I dare not let this chance pass

300's AD

John S. Langley

Haltonchesters (Onnum)

The Fort is close to where Dere Street crosses the Wall (but not at it), and spans the Wall indicating it was to house Cavalry (from Hungary). Uncommonly the Bath house is inside the Fort walls and outside there is evidence of a civilian settlement.

Our contemporary understanding of a Border is that it provides a dividing line between countries and the place where the passage of people, animals, goods, (money and tariffs/taxes) can be controlled. In wartime it can provide fortified 'dug-in' positions that the Military can operate from.

To me although the Wall seems to fulfil some of this definition the reality seems more vague and more complex; what about the networks of Roman roads, forts, settlements **North of the Wall** during these 300 years? - No wonder we have difficulty in completely understanding its function.

Shadows on the Wall

Bordering

I.

They call this a Border?

When streams and rivers and roads
run through it

When merchants bring goods and
hold Summer markets

When there are more gates than
there are soldiers now

When people drink and dance and
scream as they like

A leaky Border this and no safe place
to be after dark

Aye, and not much better in the day

And we wonder what will become of us
who chose to love Rome

Now that Rome is dwindling like mist as
a new dawn breaks

Will the lifting of one yoke bring a brighter or
a darker dawn ?

II.

Pass Friend
if you just drop a coin
into my palm
A bronze one will do

What's that
you've got there in your bag
Take it out
and let's have a look

It's tough
keeping attentive all
the day long
but if we should fail

it's all the worse
for us

300's AD

John S. Langley

Northern Lights

Deep dark the night with no Moon
is lit green in shimmering sheets
with purple streaking back to heaven
Crackling iridescence
A message from the gods

Watching eyes can only wonder
at the ethereal motion above their heads
constantly changing, brighter, darker
Shining undulations
across the starry sky

Such a spectacle must be a portent
Sent in a code to reveal warning or purpose
Stories will be made from viewing this night
Chance alone cannot
be the cause of such a thing

Wiser heads will be consulted

To translate the meaning
In their own way
In their own Time

And their word awaited
by anxious minds

300's AD

The Source

Move closer to the Source
in the hope of a clearer view
of where things originate

But is there subterfuge
gurgling beneath the moss
alternative directions

Vested interests of
the map maker's thin pen
drawing his straight lines

From afar, from above
is there a better view
or no one good spot

Only approximation
changing this way and
that at someone's will

Seek to find the Sources
to add your own spin to
the whirlpool of Truth

1600's AD

John S. Langley

Cramp

Give me blisters
That fill tight and burst
Like a balloon
Leaving agony
To walk on

Tell me the maker
Of these blister-free
promising
devil socks
has won an award

But please, please
spare me from this
Acid sharp
razor deep
Nerve slicing blades

Of pain that make
me grin involuntarily
And freeze
me rigid
In both calves

Shadows on the Wall

Who called this 'cramp'?
It is a word not strong enough
World's end
Witches curse
Would better suit

Pass me the mineral drink
Let me tough it out
Hero-like
Uncomplaining
Hoping to walk again

Tomorrow

John S. Langley

Manoeuvres

The jets engines roar
their exercises overhead
Making me duck uselessly
but instinctively

They move so fast that
their sound reaches my ears
after they have moved on
rushing through clouds

When I see them they
are like grey darts or arrows
Sleekly piecing the air
held aloft by speed

The only hindrance to
their aerodynamics are the
finned missiles that I glimpse
two under each wing

This is a deadly bird
in a peaceful sky

2000's AD

Meeting with Ghosts

There are Ghosts on the Road
Laughing together as they pass by
From the mist there are voices
drifting incoherently in a lost language

A mysterious thing,
the fog dampens ordinary senses
whilst enhancing others that
reach out from one world through the diaphanous veil

These are Ghosts on the Wall
Lives lived, journeys completed too soon
Whose lessons are largely lost
leaving us to repeatedly learn our mistakes

Laughing as they pass
Returning to the mist
Job Done

2000's AD

Rudchester (Vindobala)

The Fort was probably for both Infantry and Cavalry with troops coming from Holland. Here is another of the locations with evidence of a Mithraeum.

The Fort seems to have had a patchy time; burnt down at the end of the 100's, then re-built only to be abandoned in the late 200's, reoccupied in the late 300's.

Fire must have been of constant concern, with so many sources of open flame; torches, ovens, hearths, furnaces - I wonder if they had a 'fire brigade'?

Shadows on the Wall

John S. Langley

The Good Times

There could be laughter

There was food
and enough of it

Clothing to suit the Climate

Clear the Rules
made to play by

Baths and Latrines for hygiene

Paved roads for
ironed hoof and wheel

Warmed and lit by fiery flame

Writing, plays,
literature

Love, families and children

Hospitals
and sharp edged knives.

You've never had it so good

As the coin says
Felicis Temporis Reparatio

Happy Days are Here Again!!

Enjoy it while
you have the chance

300's AD

John S. Langley

Used Coins

This Emperor does not age yet wears thin
on the gaming table, passing between
many hands in just one night

And slips from drunken fingers to be lost
for centuries, hard won with trowel on
knees caking in slippy mud

Do we now look more closely for meaning in
crafted reverse than you did if purpose
was only to spend on more

Beer
or Bread

300's AD

Woad

She has gone
Good luck to her
For if I should find her
A knife will dig deep and spill
life's blood to empty

A simple task
To paint an Eagle
with their conjured dye
At the top of my arm in return
for hard-earned denarii

How they turn
a yellow weed
into a blue staining
paste I do not know and care less
The work was done

John S. Langley

in the firelight
and she grinning
black left quickly after
And it is now to howling laughter
that I see clear

that my Eagle
has three strange feet
with broken claws askew
and I am called 'tri-ped' the clumsy
in my own room

And worst of all
it will not take
the hot water's cleansing
I am cursed ; let her run far for
if I find her ....

300's AD

Snow

It hasn't happened so often here
The White Stuff
Falling so thick
And so quietly

Covering everything so deep
The horses
cannot get out
and we are stuck fast

Icicles hang long from the roof
dripping cold
into our bones
Whilst the blue sky laughs

At our shivering hooded forms
Huddled round
fires for warmth
Wringing our hands

300's AD

John S. Langley

Storm

See the Bright finger of Jupiter
Split the sky in forks of light
that strike to the ground
ripping gnarled trunks
in two
into flame

Feel the rain pouring from above
from the black heavy clouds
Pounding your back
Breaking your spirit
in two
into water

Shadows on the Wall

Hear the crash of awaited Thunder
Hammer of the high heavens
Shaking the Earth
Threatening to split
in two
solid ground

Wishing for the Tempest to pass
For Arcus to salve the storm
with a gentle bridge
in Rainbow colours
bringing
her message

Of Hope

300's AD

John S. Langley

Merlin

The air pulls through feathers lifting
lifting
lifting
above the hard ground
into soft air
full of dangers

The years pull through veins pulsing
pulsing
pulsing
surviving harder times
into clearer air
full of dangers

...... and imagination

Hail the chaser of sparrows
The agile one
on speedy and determined wing

Your black eyes as silver sharp
as your talons
Beware that look, it brings death

My lady asks me 'catch you' to
train you to wrist
Tame your magic for sport and games

Make the most of the time my friend
Enjoy your freedom
For I cannot delay for more than a day

800's AD

Benwell (Hill) (Condercum)

Built through the Wall (for Infantry/Cavalry from Northern Spain, Germany) Benwell had a large civilian settlement that and is now ironically buried under the current one.

There is evidence that the local coal outcrops were utilised by the Blacksmiths, and there are the remains of a Vallum Crossing still visible.

Also, by serendipity, there are the remains of the only known Temple to local god Antenociticus.

Here we can imagine the smell of the horses, neighing, sweating, steaming in their stables; the rich source of manure straw mixed, feeding the fields, increasing the yields of emmer made into the bread that fed the troops. A Roman ecosystem

Shadows on the Wall

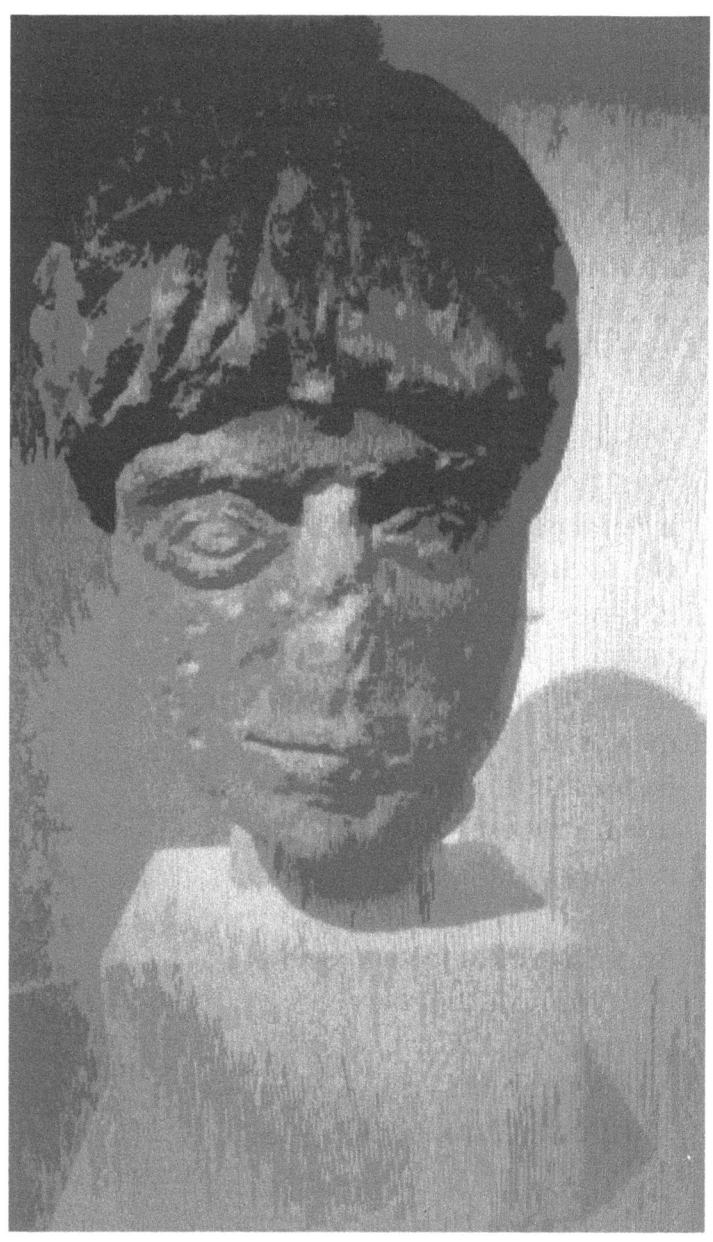

John S. Langley

A Request

Let Sleep bring a new reality
when you close your eyes
Another parallel dimension
as real as any other where time
stands and flies simultaneously

Let your sleep bring soft comfort to
your body and mind heal
by processes operating
out of day night time with your
dreams your private anaesthetic

Let no nightmares disturb slumber
meant to salve your heart
Designated home to emotions
brimming over the cup edge
in your fight for continuance

And if you do not wake to look
into your Mother's eyes
let your soul slip peacefully
into a different light
without looking back

300's AD

The Farmer

Looking up at
the clank of metal
Harsh words from
harsh mouths

Let them all pass,
back to their dice
their drink and
their women

Nod and defer to
the sharp sword edge
But spit at
their backs

Let their shadows
disappear and
return to
the land

Tilling the crops
It is you that
know of life
not them

300's AD

John S. Langley

The Auxiliary

Wherever I go I take
my own history
with me
My look, my walk
tells of my land

But here away from home
I feel more strongly
more proud
of my own roots
than I ever did

Here I am more than
I could have been back
there I
am conqueror
not conquered

and must make people
proud that their true son
protects
Rome's Standard here
At the edge of the World

300's AD

Witching Hours

All quiet
Nothing moves
The stillness settled like dew
Creeps across my skin
Raising hairs

Too quiet
A warning
Senses honed to sharpness
Standing frozen Watch
Listening

And out there
A sheep barks
Cows rip and chew the grassy cud
Time slips slowly away

Too
Too
Slowly

Towards Dawn

300'S AD

Newcastle upon Tyne (Pons Aelius)

Newcastle (the name derived from its first Norman Castle built in 1080) — city of my misspent youth — was previously called Monkchester and in Roman times was home to the Legions and also to Auxiliaries from the Cheshire, Staffordshire, and Shropshire region — the only British fort garrison on the Wall.

The Fort was not attached to the Wall and lies between it and the River Tyne. The Roman Bridge spanning the river giving source to the Latin name.

I have no doubt that this was a vibrant place even then and I'd like to pay tribute to the boilers of clothes, the bringers of fuel, the takers of ash, the unrecorded ones, the taken-for-granteds, let's give them a moment back in the Sun - take a bow, good stuff guys!
- There could not have been any sustainable socio-Wall communities without you.

Shadows on the Wall

John S. Langley

Population Explosion

Picture the walls slowly growing up
from the staid ruins
Hear the roaring of stone on stone
Experience the smells
of cooking
body odour
sweet perfumes and decay

More sounds now, feet on paving shuffling
A chatter of noise
hard iron shod hooves are clattering
See all the strange people
So many
Different
types of skin, hair and dress

All speaking, moving, milling, mixing
Seemingly random
but each intent on their journey
Taste the air, gravy thick
with living
How empty
before but now how full

Looking on with a mind's eye open
peering down alleys
squinting at what there might have been
Feeling one more time how
Different
how foreign
how familiar it is

The thousands of people the Forts with
a population
density several times that
of our Greater London a
Roman led
explosion
in these important parts

For a Time

Note: *During the Roman Times there were bustling Towns and high localised population densities e.g inside a Fort there would have been approx 36,000 people/km² compared to 2000's AD Greater London at 5,500 people/km² (a slightly unfair comparison but you get the idea).*

300's AD

John S. Langley

Bureaucrat

Lying on my silken couch
my wine diluted by my slaves
who must also taste my food
in these troubled times

What I do I do for Rome
for my family and few friends
it is not my fault that I
can kill with a word

My wishes are enacted
by others as I do not want
to soil my hands nor to join
the gawping masses

I get reports and smile or
chastise as is my wont attuned
to the capricious temper
of my full stomach

Shadows on the Wall

There is no time to go out
into wilder quarters as I
have meetings in the Baths and
dinners to attend

It is no easy matter
to endlessly make decisions
whilst always watching your back
against friend and foe

who can act alike in the
turbulence of current events
I must do unto others
and not be done to

After all
I am a servant of Rome
I owe it to her

400's AD

John S. Langley

A Mother's Prayer

Spin the sowing wheel
and make the unique thread
of her destiny

For life in this World
of the Three Worlds tied tight
by long Ashen roots

Touch my child with Good
let her grow wise as tears
from Odin's lost eye

Bring not a troubled
influence to this crib
of my own first born

Born of pain and my
blood brought into sunlight
from my open womb

Let her drink deeply
of the wide Well of Fate
and grant her a better

Life

Than her Mother's

1000's AD

The Wind

How many sounds has the Wind
up here on a whistling dark night
Powerful, Strong
Pressing, Heavy
Icy Gusts

Fanning the fires flames to sparks
The tendril smoke to turbulence
Fresh, Bitter, Brisk,
Fierce, Chill, Sharp,
Biting

Feel the violence roar menace
Raw and Wild, Furious, Angry
Bleak, Terrible
Harsh as a
dice roll

1200's AD

John S. Langley

The Interview

I'll tell you what this is
It is this
I'll tell you how they did it
'Twas like this

They had talents and skills
evidently
Far beyond their time that we
lost for a while

No they were not smarter nor
as civilised
as we who have climbed on
their shoulders

We are the master race
What's that?
You say they said that once?
Ah yes, but we are right

1700's AD

Pilgrimages

When many centuries had passed
and there were leisure hours to be found
We turned our eyes our heads around
To look back on our own land's past

And after years of contemplation
Of walking miles in rain, snow or shine
And talking it over with a glass of wine
We thought a thorough exploration

Would be an instructive thing to do
And so in 1849
We did set forth, the first of our time
To traverse the Wall tho we were few

We never thought that a century on
and more, that what we did would be
remembered never mind that the
pilgrimages would be still going strong

If we had thought maybe we should
not have started

Note: *(It cannot be taken for granted that these 19th century gentlemen would be happy with the number of visitors to the Wall in the 21st century)*

1800's AD

John S. Langley

On Their Shoulders

Gildas, Camden, Stukeley,
Gale, Clayton, Hodgson,
Horsley, MacLauchlan,

Bruce, Collingwood, Birley
Breeze, Dobson, Hutton,
Warburton, Bede

Just some of the people
we turn to
for understanding

Shadows on the Wall

Because the Romans are
not around
to ask

And no Operating
Manual
has been left behind

And then there's us
When we go
we each leave a trace

That says
We were here too

500-2000 AD

Wallsend (Segedunum)

Where there triumphal statues of Hadrian at each end of the Wall – larger than life, covered in Gold? Emperors were not in general shy of putting their personal stamp on their achievements; especially as they were on their way to becoming gods.

The Fort spanned the Wall and there is evidence of Cavalry from Eastern France. It was probably not the original terminus of the Wall (that was probably at Newcastle) but the Wall was extended and went down to meet the River East of the Fort.

The Fort was submerged under housing that has since been demolished to reveal the remains that can be seen today, with elevated viewing and reconstructed Bath House. The view of Shipyard cranes peering over Roman remains is iconic.

Close by a section of Wall has been reconstructed to its guessed original height and castellated top – giving a very clear idea of how imposing and impregnable it would have appeared (especially if were rendered and painted white as is one possibility).

The Wall didn't really end rather it merged with the wider infrastructure; piers and boats linking the Land and River/Sea communication and transport lanes.

Shadows on the Wall

Father to Son

Every Journey Starts
With the First Step

Followed
By Another

Each New Step
Is a Journey

Note: *After generations have been born on the Wall the leaving is now in the opposite direction.*

400'S AD

Alienation

I will bury my grief
in the ground of my enemies

in this foreign soil
that is putrid in my hands

Slipping through my fingers
dirt that has tarnished my life

Let the bitters that I taste
be transformed to acid

that burns to the heart of this place
and devours its foul soul

I have never hated place more
I want to be away before

I am consumed

400's AD

John S. Langley

Wall's End

The journey ends at an End
Wallsend

Time flows
Like the waters of the Tyne

Past and passing
We have seen but may not see
the next tide

As we drift on

We have been a part
A small part
Our part

And that's enough
That has to be enough

400's AD

What's in a Name

I.

Vallum Aelium
The Pict's Wall
Severus' Wall
Hadrian's Wall
Clayton's rebuilt Wall
Turf Wall
Stone Wall
Broad Foundation Wall
Narrow Foundation Wall
Vallum Hadriani
The Roman Wall

II.

Wall of hope
of fear
of longing
to leave

Wall of tears
of life
of water
to run

Wall of walls
of stone
of stories
of earth

III.

Lots of names
But at least
I think we agree
it is a Wall

21st Century Travel

So now the whole Wall line
can be travelled in a day
By families with picnics
buying ice creams
even in the rain

Seeing more in one day
than was possible in a
lifetime when the Wall was tall
with foreboding
even in the rain

Each knew enough to get
by so perhaps we hunt for
more knowledge than they needed
to live their lives
even in the rain

2000's AD

John S. Langley

Will?

Will the World be ever steady?
I have seen eight Emperors come and go
Though we still spend their coin
covered in out-of-date messages
that make us laugh
but still buy bread
A Metal legacy
tarnished or to be transmogrified

Will the Wall be ever steady?
It has seen eighteen centuries come and go
Though we can still define the path
It's peak has been long past and lost
that makes us think
what might have been
A Stone legacy
hardy but hardly indestructible

Shadows on the Wall

Will the Word be ever steady?
Even when Languages and truths come and go
Though we still find an imprint
covered in contemporary messages
They talked as we talk
of the same things
A Literary legacy
fragile relics yielding immortality

Will the World be ever steady?
As the Ball spins and eons come and go
Though we still spend our time
sending out-of-date messages
that would make others laugh
now asleep in their bed
A Human legacy
rotting back to blacken the fertile Earth

100-2000's AD

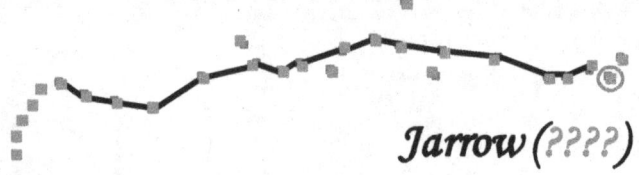

Jarrow (????)

Jarrow's place in the Roman World is uncertain and no Latin name has been identified that can be confidently ascribed to it. There is some suggestion that there was a 1st Century Roman Fort here and because of its position with respect to Newcastle, South Shields and the River I've chosen to believe this.

Its name is a corruption of the Old English word for 'Marsh Dwellers' giving some idea of the type of terrain that was then extant.

It is, of course, famous for its association with the Venerable Bede (the Monastery at Jarrow was his home in the 700's); who is regarded as the greatest Anglo-Saxon scholar and the father of English history (his writings including reference to the Roman Wall)

From the mid 1800's Jarrow was also well known as a centre for shipbuilding with Warships, Fishing Boats, Cargo vessels all built and launched from here.

Shadows on the Wall

John S. Langley

Language

They speak strangely here
the local people
I can speak several tongues
but their accent can defeat me

They laugh uproariously
at things I don't get
and grin and wink in a language
beyond talking without speaking

It is very annoying

I am their superior

but they give me little respect

I thought they would learn

That I would make sure of it

and their grinning would cease

But they see my irritation and smile

Aaaaaaargh.......

400's AD

Formulae

There is a form for everything
Our Bureaucracy and Administration rule
If you want to get ahead
get a form!

Even the gods love a routine
'willingly and deservedly fulfilled his vow'
must complete the stone Altar
raised in thanks

In requesting leave I must beg
that I be considered as 'a worthy person'
and smile deferentially
and grovel

There is a rule for everything
From Birth to Death, for getting Paid, for being Sick
I'm just so grateful
that I'm a Freed Man !

400's AD

John S. Langley

Omens

Green flames tearing up the Night Sky
A White Stag in the Light of the Moon
A Raven cawing Three Times
A Black Snake slithering under the Wall
Wolves howling at noon
A star falling trailing fire to the Earth
Dice that throw 7 time and again

I tell you
I have seen these things
It does not bode well

400's AD

Marsh Dwellers

I. Roman Fort

First century walls
mark the coming of Right Angles
jarring wrong in a circular world

South of the River
Made as a safe sanctuary
To await the Emperor's pleasure

A fleeting visit
to give an imperial command
for a more widely stretching project

II. **Bede**

Surviving the plague was harder
than writing about Cuthbert
To sing the Service of Liturgy
holding the fort until others
could come
at 14

The thousands of donated beasts
a nurtured crop of vellum
to record in Latin the Gospel
from this Centre of Learning
sent out
to the World

Shadows on the Wall

With respect for who went before
Roman and Greek writers
Made Histories telling of unity
whether wished for or more real
written
in clear style

Risked Heracy through applied maths
by re-calculating
the age of the Earth more wrong and less
right than was permitted to say
out loud
in his Time

Coelwulf, King of Northumbria
was patron in this age of
Miracles where Cuthbert accepted
Rome and whose body lay incorrupt
after death
eleven years

Hermit, healer and worker of Miracles
Saint of the North

III. **Shipbuilding**

Warships, Cargo vessels
Fishing boats for the prime Tyne eels
A fleet more than a thousand strong
and built to last

A short 80 years and
200 march South in protest
An invasion from the North East
not be ignored

Not to be ignored
Not the time to be ignored
Pride, time and Perseverance
Should Never be ignored

100-1900 AD

John S. Langley

South Shields (Arbeia)

Laying on the South bank and at the mouth of the River Tyne the site was occupied with Round House and Cultivation 4000 years before the Romans arrived.

In the Roman Fort there is evidence of layers of change to suit the varying needs of differing Times and Infantry from France, Cavalry from Hungary and SW Spain, Seamen from Iraq are all evidenced here.

At its peak as a Supply Base at least 22 granaries were present; the Sea, Harbour and River thoroughfares for the movement of goods and equipment, troops and traders.

A large civilian settlement was (of course) associated with the Fort and Emperors (Caracalla, Geta ...) probably sailed to/from here.

Destroyed by fire in approximately 300 AD and rebuilt; ships wrecked off the not-always-calm coast; ravaged later by the Danes (Vikings); built over in the 1800's; houses demolished in the 1900's; remains revealed through Archaeological excavation; reconstructions built to further memory and recapture some understanding – this is/was a place to be reckoned with.

Shadows on the Wall

Granary at Night

Patiently the cat waits
Silent in the dark
Listening for Rats

Black
that gnaw through hessian
to feed on plump grain

A noise
Scurry stop
Scurry stop
Sniff

The cat waits
Head turns
Eyes seek

Patiently
Patiently

There is food
Aplenty
Here

Luck and Fate

Six sided temptress

Decider of Futures
Bringer of Fortune
Feller of Dreams
Dealer of Despair
Dasher of Hopes
Maiden of Chance

Transport me into Sunshine
In this

my last throw of the Dice

400's AD

Picking over the Ruins

Broken stone is scattered that
once were walls
high strong impregnable
now laid low by time and robbery

Clambering along in single file
looking only at feet
for a safer footing
not looking up or back but down

Other's footsteps have indented
the ancient surface
polished and worn it
to a smoothness made for slipping

and as our feet echo back we walk
a different path
Hoping for more solid ground
amongst the shifting sands

North Sea Coast

The Sea in lines of breaking white
rolls across the silent shore
No-one to watch the water's might
immutable as the tides roar

Rising, falling to the Moon's beat
Like, unlike Britannia's fate
tribally bearing the Roman fleet
on Time's time to navigate

No looking back, no memory
Of yesterday's flat waters
Salt sands washed clean; of history
no flotsam woos the watchers

Stern of a ship disappearing
dipping, rising and falling flight
Away from a round Sun rising
throwing stars of sparkling light

that flash brilliant and are gone

400'S AD

John S. Langley

Red Sky

Over my shoulder
I feel the crimson touch
of the setting Sun

I will not turn to look
It is too late

If it augurs ill or well
I will leave to the gods of chance
The diviners of the future

I am leaving
My life road stretches ahead

I have no need,
It does no good
To look back

400's AD

And now where to?

We have the open Sea, the Eastern Coastline; it's difficult to know where to stop so let's not bring our trip to a conclusion but rather take a pause.......

.... on a journey that does not need to end.

John S. Langley

Shadows on the Wall

There is no end to this Wall
No end to the stories

Different strides
Different purposes
Will bring others

Until the stones crumble
Or the World ends

That's got to be a good thing

John S. Langley

Shadows on the Wall

This was a time of magic, of sea monsters, mystery and myth, where news travelled slowly and the only 'truth' were in the words of the news bringers themselves.

Rome had an appetite for the bizarre and what could be more curious than stories from the very edge of their terrifying world.

The views in this poem are taken from the writings of Julius Caesar, Virgil, Tacitus, Cassius Dio, Herodian, Procopius amongst others being a reflection of what they actually wrote about Britain.

It is not clear whether they all had first-hand experience or whether their views were conjured from third-hand information or moulded ('spun') to suit the 'wild, barbarian' image that went down well in 'civilised' Rome.

(With homage and apologies to the 'Lambton Worm')

John S. Langley

Truth

For those of you who sit in Rome
and will never venture there
I bring you news of our farthest lands
enough to curl your hair

Sit quietly now and listen in
I'll tell you all the awful story
Sit quietly now and listen in
I'll tell you about the Wall

There's many felt inclined to go
And fight in foreign lands
And join a troop of valiant friends
That fear not wounds nor scars

But don't go off to this here Land
Where queer things do befall
They're painted Blue and eat raw meat
That live yon side o'the Wall

The people there are giant sized
Proficient with spears and knives
They hide in bogs up to their necks
And share their kids and wives

Shadows on the Wall

They inhabit high high mountains
and desolate swampy plains
they live on flocks and donkeys
and don't use loos or drains

Dwelling in tents they are naked
but fierce and dangerous when riled
Thick mist wraps all around them
the atmosphere's gloomy and wild

And, strangest of all, the inhabitants say
that if any man crosses the Wall
he'll die straightaway in a moment
with no friend to hear his last call

These fearful folk will often feed
on calves and lambs and sheep,
and swallow little children
when they've gone off to sleep

And when they've stolen all they can
and made bad waste of it all
They crawl away and disappear
to the North of the towering Wall

But if we catch these less than beasts
we cut them into halves
and that stops them from eating kids
and chicks and lambs and calves

So now you know how all us folks
on our South side of the Wall
lose lots of sheep and lots of sleep
defending our Roman call

Now you can go off to yer beds
and think about the awful story
Now you can go off to yer beds
and dream about the Wall

www.ingramcontent.com/pod-product-compliance
Lightning Source LLC
Chambersburg PA
CBHW011957090526
44590CB00023B/3757